Lighting The Way To God

Lighting The Way To God

**Giving People a Context
for Understanding the Gospel**

JAMES A. ODENS

Lighting the Way to God

Copyright © 1999 by James A. Odens

Published by TCBS
4233 Edgemont Street
Vadnais Heights, MN 55127-7946

All rights reserved. No part of this publication may be reproduced, stored in a retrieval system or transmitted in any form by any means, electronic, mechanical, photocopy, recording or otherwise, without the prior permission of the publisher, except as provided by USA copyright law.

Unless otherwise indicated, Bible quotations are taken from *The New American Standard Bible*, copyright © 1960, 1962, 1963, 1968, 1971, 1972, 1975, 1977, and 1995 by The Lockman Foundation, and are used by permission.

Cover design: Adam Turner Visuals

ISBN: 0-9627088-1-X

Library of Congress Catalog Card Number 99-90126

To Sean Helmes

I love you, child of my child. It is my prayer that the way to God will be fully lit before you, and that by His grace you will follow that path as a passionate seeker of truth.

Table of Contents

Preface	ix
Acknowledgements	xiii

Part One
Theocentric Evangelism

Chapter 1:	What is Theocentric Evangelism?	19
Chapter 2:	Why is Theocentric Evangelism Necessary?	25
Chapter 2:	How to Evangelize Theocentrically	39

Part Two
Chronological Bible Study

Chapter 4:	What is Evangelistic Chronological Bible Study?	47
Chapter 5:	Why is Chronological Bible Study Needed in Evangelism?	51
Chapter 6:	What to Expect when Studying the Bible Chronologically in Evangelism	67

Part Three
Using Theocentric Chronological Bible Studies in Evangelism

Chapter 7:	Prayerfully Preparing	71
Chapter 8:	Prayerfully Teaming	75
Chapter 9:	Prayerfully Planning	81
Chapter 10:	Prayerfully Inviting	85
Chapter 11:	Prayerfully Conducting the Sessions	89
Chapter 12:	Prayerfully Concluding the Study	95
Chapter 13:	Prayerfully Following Up	97

Conclusion: Oak Trees or Squash   99

Preface

Philip exemplifies what this book is all about. Having just met Jesus and responded to His command to follow Him, Philip locates his friend Nathaniel and says to him, "We have found Him of whom Moses in the law and also the Prophets wrote—Jesus of Nazareth, the son of Joseph." When Nathaniel questions the possibility of his claim, Philip's response is a simple, "Come and see" (John 1:43-46).

Notice what is taking place here. Philip cannot contain his excitement over the fact that he met the Redeemer whom God promised to Israel for so many centuries. He just has to tell his buddy! This news is too good, too important, too thrilling to keep quiet. God has been faithful to His Word again!

The focus of Philip's announcement is on Jesus, God the Son. His purpose is to point Nathaniel to the Nazarene as the one about whom God spoke often in His Word through Moses and the prophets. His method is to relate Jesus of Nazareth to what God had previously revealed in the Scriptures.

Of course, Philip had it easy in one respect. Nathaniel already knew what God said through Moses and the Prophets about His coming Redeemer. Philip didn't have to tell him about those things. Rather, he just needed to refer to them and Nathaniel knew what he was saying. After all, Nathaniel had been studying the Scriptures since early boyhood, constantly hearing and reading about the Redeemer whom God first promised in Genesis 3:15.

That luxury for Philip is rarely available today. The problem is not merely with the Biblical illiteracy of our culture in general. Evangelical believers themselves are largely illiterate when it comes to understanding the background to the gospel of God provided in Old Testament Scriptures.

How do I know this is the case? Because when I talk to Christians about giving people a context to understand the gospel by presenting the Old Testament background to it, they tell me they can't because they don't know that background themselves!

This is not an isolated incident. In 1998 I traveled the United States from coast to coast, conducting seminars and church conferences about theocentric, chronological evangelism. Everywhere I went and every time I spoke, dear Christians would confess their ignorance of the context for the gospel provided by God in the Old Testament. They wanted to go through a chronological Bible study themselves before taking nonbelievers through one, and rightly so!

While a chronological approach to the Scriptures is vital in providing a context for understanding the gospel, it must be undertaken from a theocentric perspective. The gospel must be centered in the person and work of God. It starts with Him and it ends with Him.

It is one thing for me, the messenger, to "do all things for the sake of the gospel, so that I may become a fellow partaker of it" (1 Corinthians 9:23). To become as a Jew, as one under the Law, as one without the Law, or as one who is weak in order to relate to those who are such is a commendable ministry approach. It is simply a matter of relating to those I am reaching with the gospel of God.

However, we must not allow anything to change the message of the gospel. Unfortunately, that is what is happening in the evangelical church today. As Christopher Sugden warns, "contextualisation of the gospel can become over-contextualisation," and this results in "shaping the gospel"[1] that is being presented.

---

[1] Christopher Sugden, "Modernity, Postmodernity and the Gospel," *Transformation*, October, 1993, p. 2.

One way this takes place is by allowing our presentation of the gospel to become consumer-driven. Because our hearers take offense at the idea of a God who calls for perfect obedience and pours out His wrath on sinners, we play down or even omit references to God that present Him in that way.

Because our audiences want to maintain a high "self-esteem" and "self-image," we are reluctant to point out sin and call for repentance. Because they are completely self-centered, we let our message revolve around them instead of around God.

Such was not the case in the evangelism of the early church. In section one of this book we will examine the messages of the apostles and other servants of God in Acts. You will notice immediately that their proclamation was focused on God and unrelenting in its call for repentance and faith in His Son.

This was not because the Biblical messengers were unaware or unconcerned about the felt needs of their audiences. To the contrary, they were keenly interested in the personal situations of the people to whom they ministered. However, they addressed these personal issues as a steppingstone to the gospel, and the personal issues were never allowed to affect the content of the gospel they preached or their basic approach in presenting that gospel.

Therefore, when the apostles Peter and John came upon a lame man, he was made whole and leaped around rejoicing. However, he then listened to Peter proclaim a powerful message calling for repentance, one directed toward himself as much as the rest of the crowd (Acts 3).

The format of this book reflects the desires driving it. First and foremost, my prayer is that believers will see what it means to be God-centered in daily life and, as a result, in evangelistic ministry. Those two aspects of the Christian life are inseparable.

Secondly, I pray you will see the immeasurable value of taking a chronological Bible study approach to evangelism, thereby giving people a context for understanding the precious gospel of God. Then, once you have chosen to adopt this approach, I hope to use the experiences and observations we have made over the years to help you in carrying out a theocentric, chronological evangelistic ministry, reaching your world with the gospel.

May God deign to use this tool for the growth and strengthening of His kingdom, to the praise of the glory of His grace in Christ Jesus.

Acknowledgements

I am the grateful beneficiary of the efforts of many others who have played major roles in discovering and developing the principles and suggestions about which you will read in this book. However, all of them will join me in confessing that anything of value here is from God, and what is not of God is of no worth at all. So we exclaim with the apostle Paul, "Oh, the depth of the riches both of the wisdom and knowledge of God! How unsearchable are His judgments and unfathomable His ways!" (Romans 11:33).

Other than the Lord Himself, no one knows better than my wife Jill and our daughters Kim, Kara and Kristi how much I desire to be completely God-centered in my life, and how often I come far short of this goal. Yet, by the grace of God, they, along with our son-in-law Hunter, have joined wholeheartedly with me in seeking that goal for their own lives. It is one of this life's most precious blessings to have a family of truth-seekers.

Jill has been my wife for over 25 years, and I love her passionately. She is my moon, reflecting the Sonlight to me when my nights get dark. She is my Bathnabas, a daughter of encouragement willing to support me in my "impossible" dreams. One of the greatest miracles in my life has been how God has worked in us, melding two completely different persons and giving us a singular zeal for delighting in the God who is enough.

My parents, Arthur and Marie Odens, raised me to think theocentrically. God was the focus of life for them, not just for verbal evangelism. With such a heritage, I praise God for entrusting me to their care, along with my six siblings, and for empowering them to fulfill their stewardship over us as our parents.

Among the multitude of people God has used in bringing

about this book are Jim and Jill, the young couple with whom I held my first chronological Bible study years ago—at their request! It is both humbling and thrilling that God would use a nonbelieving (at the time) couple to open the eyes of a young pastor, asking him to give them a context for understanding the gospel by starting at the beginning and taking them through the Bible chronologically! The fact that they have the same first names as my wife and I have causes me to remember them with even greater fondness.

Among the many preachers and authors the Lord has used to influence me in relation to the themes of this book, there are two whom I must mention by name. John MacArthur's book *Our Sufficiency in Christ*,[1] though written to address the evangelical Church's capitulation to the onslaught of psychology, pragmatism and mysticism, and to remind the Church that we have all we need in Christ, was a valuable encouragement to me, reinforcing my belief that evangelism must be blatantly theocentric. When someone sees from the beginning that God is enough, that new Christian is less likely to yield to the temptation of looking elsewhere for fulfillment or solutions.

More recently, I have been thrilled to interact with John Piper through his books reflecting the Biblical truth of what he calls *Christian hedonism*. Two of them will be referenced in a footnote early in this book. A complete listing of Piper's writings and available sermons may be found on the Desiring God web site, www.desiringGOD.org . I encourage you to look it up and read as much of what he has written as you can afford.

Then there are the many team members with whom I have been privileged to serve alongside as we ministered the gospel of

---

[1] John F. MacArthur, Jr., *Our Sufficiency in Christ* (Dallas: Word Publishing, 1991).

God to friends, neighbors, relatives and fellow workers through chronological Bible studies. I have learned much from every team and every study we have held, and count it an honor to have been associated with each Christian on each team. Every time I get involved in a new evangelistic study, I am excited over what God will do in me through the team, just as much as over what He will do in the lives of those to whom we are ministering the gospel.

PART ONE

THEOCENTRIC EVANGELISM

CHAPTER ONE

What is Theocentric Evangelism?

Theocentric evangelism is ministering the gospel of God to the lost in such a way that the focus is on Him. A theocentric approach to evangelism emphasizes who God is and what God does. His person and activity are set forth as the foundation and driving force which motivates and enables any response called for on the part of the hearers, including trusting Christ.

The best way to grasp theocentric evangelism is to contrast it with its alternative approach to evangelism, the anthropocentric (man-centered) approach. In doing so, we can point out the differences in these approaches in four areas.

The Goal of Redemption

In theocentric evangelism, God is viewed as the means and the end of redemption. Salvation is not only completely designed and carried out by God, but also His ultimate purpose in it is understood to be His glory. Redemption is seen as a major part of God's program to "be all in all" (1 Corinthians 15:28).

A man-centered approach to evangelizing presents God more as the means to an end. The end in mind may be any number of things: heaven, peace of mind, freedom from feelings of guilt, etc. Usually these ends are worthwhile goals. In fact, they are often scripturally valid as immediate or secondary ends.

However, anthropocentric evangelism presents them as primary ends of redemption by default, focusing attention on them and failing to demonstrate God's glory as the ultimate, primary goal.

The Source of Happiness

One's understanding of the goal of redemption determines in great part what he views as the source of happiness, and vice versa. God-centered evangelism offers happiness in God. He is considered the sum, substance and source of all true joy. Knowing Him is eternal life (John 17:3). Any blessings He gives people are recognized as object lessons teaching the truth that our all-sufficiency is in Him, the Giver, rather than in the blessings He provides.

In contrast, man-centered evangelism offers happiness in what God provides. This may include streets of gold, freedom from fear, provision of material needs, physical health, or a multitude of other blessings from God. Of course, no Christian actually tells a nonbeliever that these things are the source of happiness. It's just that many times in our evangelism, we focus on the blessings rather than on the Blessed One who gives them. We entice people to come to God for what they will receive from Him, and they seldom, if ever, hear that it is God in whom true happiness and joy are found.

In other words, too often we don't take people deeper than the surface where they have been living their lives all along. We talk about how God will give them this and that and the other thing, but don't lead people to realize that He is all they need.

Consider for a moment how Jesus ministered to the woman at the well of Sychar, an encounter described for us in John 4:3-26. He started the discussion on a subject with which she was highly familiar—asking her for a drink of water (v. 7). Then He raised the conversation to a higher level, offering to give her living water that would spring up to eternal life (vs. 10-14).

However, Jesus did not stop there! After demonstrating His supernatural knowledge and pointing out her sinful lifestyle (vs. 15-18), He drew her attention to God the Father and Himself as the Messiah. (vs. 21-26). True worship of God was the ultimate issue in this conversation, not water! If this woman was to be truly happy, it would not be because she never needed to return to the well again. It would be because she knew God, whom to know is eternal life.

This Biblical account is a perfect pattern for the approach we should be taking in our evangelistic endeavors. Felt needs and desired blessings are fine for a starting point, as attention-getting devices and ice-breakers. However, we must go much deeper if we aspire to be faithful to the gospel of God.

The Purpose of Life

From a theocentric perspective, the purpose for which mankind was created is to glorify God as the God who is enough. We fulfill our reason for existence by finding in Him our total ecstasy and absolute joy. We are complete when we depend solely and fully on Him and find Him to be more than all we could ask or think. Life is full when our only desire is to know Him better, when our major frustration is that "we see in a mirror dimly" (1 Corinthians 13:12).

With this understanding of the purpose of life, the essence of man's problem is recognized as our failure to glorify Him as God (Romans 1:21). Whenever we seek to find ultimate fulfillment or happiness in someone or something other than God Himself, we have violated our reason for existence. When we depend on self or substance, we dishonor Him for whose glory we were formed.

Man-centered religion, at its best, portrays life's purpose as being to appease God as the God who expects more. The focus is not on His all-sufficiency, but on our insufficiency, our inability to please Him. God is pictured as a spoiled despot whose anger falls on us simply because we don't always do what He wants. The concern is not with the fact that God is not honored as the God who is enough, but rather is with the consequences such a failure brings on the sinner.

The Nature of Salvation

In a theocentric presentation of the gospel, salvation is described in terms of God's complete deliverance of man from sin, with equal emphasis on every aspect of that deliverance. God's justification of believers, declaring us righteous, results in salvation from the penalty we deserve for our sin—unending separation from God. Justification is a completed event for believers in every respect, giving us "peace with God through our Lord Jesus Christ" (Romans 5:1).

God also sanctifies His own, a present and continuing process of conforming us to the image of His Son as we continue in this life. It is how He works out in us His deliverance from the power of sin over us. Finally, God glorifies believers, a future reality for which we wait with eagerness, for at that time His deliverance from the presence of sin will become an accomplished fact in our lives.

Because man-centered evangelism appeals more to man's comfort than God's glory and places most of the responsibility for sanctification on man rather than God, it is characterized by an emphasis on justification and glorification. Justification is presented as the means to escape "hell" and glorification as the means to enjoy the blessings of heaven. Sanctification, present deliverance from sin's power and conformity to Christ, is seldom involved in the discussion of salvation with nonbelievers, even though they are slaves of sin at the moment!

To put it another way, theocentric evangelism proclaims salvation from sin, while man-centered evangelism emphasizes salvation from sin's results. One deals with the root and includes the branches. The other waves the branches and frequently ends up wondering why the root keeps showing itself. One believes God in grace has provided a comprehensive salvation for this life and the next, while the other gives Him credit for the next life but makes it appear that He came up short in dealing with sin's power over the believer in this life.

CHAPTER TWO

Why is Theocentric Evangelism Necessary?

It would be easy to base the need for God-centered evangelism on the condition of the evangelical church in our day. For that approach, a good starting point would be David Wells' observation that God is functionally irrelevant for most evangelicals today.[1] Assuming this is true, it would seem evident that one way of dealing with this problem would be to emphasize the character and work of God while evangelizing, demonstrating His definite, total relevance in daily life in this world. Perhaps if people saw His relevance as they were first introduced to the gospel, they would be less likely to consider Him irrelevant in their Christian lives.

However, as powerful a case as this could make for theocentric evangelism, it is more pragmatic than Biblical. For our purposes, we will choose to look at three even more potent reasons calling for a return to truly God-centered evangelism by the Church of today. Consider them carefully, with an open Bible and a mind ready to engage with marvelous truths, familiar as they may be.

---

[1] Christopher Sugden, "Modernity, Postmodernity and the Gospel," *Transformation*, October, 1993, p. 2.

Because God is God!

Who can number the splendors of our holy God? He is infinitely glorious and great. As the apostle Paul exclaimed, "Oh the depth of the riches both of the wisdom and knowledge of God! How unsearchable are His judgments and unfathomable His ways!" (Romans 11:33). He reveals Himself as "The LORD, the LORD God, compassionate and gracious, slow to anger, and abounding in lovingkindness and truth; who keeps lovingkindness for thousands, who forgives iniquity, transgression and sin; yet He will by no means leave *the guilty* unpunished, visiting the iniquity of fathers on the children and on the grandchildren to the third and fourth generations" (Exodus 34:6-7).

The limitless majesty and marvelous beauty of our God is why we evangelize. In fact, in a very real sense evangelism may be considered *the activity of making known to others the glories of our God.*[2] After all, the gospel is the good news *of God*, as Paul declared in his exposition of it for the Roman believers (Romans 1:1; 15:16). In other words, the gospel is the wonderful message of who God is and what He has done to free undeserving, willful slaves of sin and make them trophies of His grace!

Paul significantly closes his paean of praise in Romans 11 by reminding us that God is the focal point of the universe and the one who will be glorified by the ultimate outworking of all events in history: "For from Him and through Him and to Him are all things. To Him *be* the glory forever. Amen" (Romans 11:36). The gospel properly understood is centered completely on God. Knowing Him is life eternal (John 17:3).

---

[2] "Evangelism is a way of revealing the universals of God's character through the particulars of everyday living." Joseph C. Aldrich, *Gentle Persuasion* (Portland, OR: Multnomah Press, 1988), p. 30.

This means any legitimate approach to evangelism will focus on making known the glories of God. Salvation is to be viewed as God's means of enabling people to fulfill the chief purpose of our existence, which is "to glorify God by enjoying Him forever."[3] This takes it far beyond a common approach of our day, which merely offers salvation as a means of "fire escape" and places the emphasis on man's comfort rather than God's glory.

Scriptural evidence abounds for the fact that God created this world and designed redemption with the ultimate purpose of glorifying Himself.[4] Among the many texts revealing this truth about creation is Psalm 104. After blessing the Lord (v. 1), the psalmist goes into a lengthy description of His universe (vs. 2-30). A clear statement of the purpose of creation follows (vs. 31-32), which leads to the response of the psalmist's God-centered heart (vs. 33-35). In the words of the psalmist, creation exists to "Let the glory of the LORD endure forever; Let the LORD be glad in His works."

The spirit world was created to glorify God. When we see the many passages that command angelic beings to glorify Him (Psalm 103:20-21; 148:2; Hebrews 1:6) combined with many more describing their worship of him (Isaiah 6:1-3; Revelation 4:8-11; 5:11-14; 7:11-12), their ultimate reason for existence is beyond question.

---

[3] John Piper, *God's Passion for His Glory* (Wheaton, IL: Crossway Books, 1998), p. 80. By means of this quotation and footnote, I commend wholeheartedly the thrust of his message contained therein and accompanied by Jonathan Edwards' treatise on "The End for Which God Created the World." Piper develops the concept of "Christian hedonism" more fully in *Desiring God: Meditations of a Christian Hedonist* (Sisters, OR: Multnomah Press, 1996).
[4] See Edwards' "The End for Which God Created the World" in John Piper, *God's Passion for His Glory* to read a more complete summation of Biblical evidence.

The natural, physical world also exists for the glory of God. In addition to Psalm 104, familiar texts such as Psalm 8 ("O LORD, our Lord, how majestic is Your name in all the earth, who have displayed Your splendor above the heavens!") and Psalm 19:1-6 ("The heavens are telling of the glory of God") make this abundantly clear.

So do passages such as Psalm 29:1-9. Here David mentions the waters, thunder, forests, lightning, and calving deer as elements of nature in which God's glory is displayed. His summary statement is that "in His temple everything says, Glory!" (v. 9). The angelic realm cannot help but respond to the splendor of God displayed in the material realm by ascribing to God the glory due His name (vs. 1-2).

As the capstone of God's creation in this world, mankind exists to glorify God. The fact that sin entered the human race in the Garden of Eden did not change the purpose for our existence. It simply meant that God would glorify Himself through man in a completely unique manner.

On one hand, God glorifies Himself through punishing sin. That punishment may be temporal, such as in Numbers 14:20-23 when God prevented unbelieving Israel from entering the land promised to them. In His words, "indeed, as I live, all the earth will be filled with the glory of the LORD. Surely all the men who have seen My glory and My signs which I performed in Egypt and in the wilderness, yet have put Me to the test these ten times and have not listened to My voice, shall by no means see the land which I swore to their fathers, nor shall any of those who spurned Me see it."

God's dealings with Sidon also evidence how He glorifies Himself through punishment of sinful people. "Behold, I am against you, O Sidon, and I will be glorified in your midst. Then they will know that I am the LORD when I execute judgments in her, and I will manifest My holiness in her" (Ezekiel 28:22-23).

The Lord's eternal punishment of sin is also designed to bring glory to Himself. This is the manifest argument of Paul in Romans 9:22, rhetorically asking, "What if God, although willing to demonstrate His wrath and to make His power known, endured with much patience vessels of wrath prepared for destruction?"

In this regard, God's dealing with man is not unique. His treatment of sinful human beings does not differ from His punishment of the angels that sinned. In fact, they will be together in the end (Matthew 25:41; Revelation 20:10, 14-15).

However, God also glorifies Himself in relation to mankind by exercising His mercy and grace in delivering sinful people. And there is no question as to God's ultimate purpose for providing deliverance. It is always in order to glorify Himself.

This is true of His deliverance from physical danger, such as Israel at the Red Sea: "Nevertheless He saved them for the sake of His name, That He might make His power known" (Psalm 106:8). It is also true of His delayed wrath on His stubborn and rebellious people: "For the sake of My name I delay My wrath, and *for* My praise I restrain it for you, in order not to cut you off.... For My own sake, for My own sake, I will act; for how can *My name* be profaned? And my glory I will not give to another" (Isaiah 48:9, 11).

Finally, that God redeems His people spiritually for the ultimate purpose of glorifying Himself is an emphasis of His Word impossible to overlook. For example, notice how He introduces His great promise of the new birth through the prophet Ezekiel, saying, "'It is not for your sake, O house of Israel, that I am about to act, but for My holy name... I will vindicate the holiness of My great name.... Then the nations will know that I am the LORD,' declares the Lord GOD, 'when I prove Myself holy among you in their sight'" (Ezekiel 36:22-23).

At the same time Paul speaks of God enduring with much

patience the vessels of wrath prepared for destruction (Romans 9:22), he continues by adding that *"He did so* to make known the riches of His glory upon vessels of mercy, which He prepared beforehand for glory, *even* us, whom He also called, not from among Jews only, but also from among Gentiles" (Romans 9:23-24). His mercy and grace toward us is certainly for our good, but it is ultimately for His honor and praise.

In Ephesians 1:3-14 Paul opens his letter by outlining the roles of the triune God in redemption, as a means of praising God. His conclusion of each segment is a key element of the apostle's message. God the Father acted in redemption "to the praise of the glory of His grace" (Ephesians 1:6). The Beloved Son fulfilled His role in redemption that believers might be "to the praise of His glory" (Ephesians 1:12). Finally, the Holy Spirit of promise serves as the pledge of our inheritance "to the praise of His glory" (Ephesians 1:14).

Those whom God delivers from the ravages of sin are enabled by His indwelling Spirit to actively glorify Him in this life through our speech (Romans 15:5-6), conduct (Matthew 5:16; 1 Corinthians 6:20; 1 Peter 2:12), and even our death (John 21:19). In the next life, it only gets better, as we serve and worship Him in a perfect environment (Revelation 15:2-4; 22:3-5)!

When these passages are combined with the many others in Scripture, we cannot escape the reality that everything points ultimately to the glory of God. Our evangelistic approach must reflect this truth and our evangelistic message must declare it. This demands a theocentric approach to evangelism in which God is our focus, not man.

Because Jesus is Lord!

Matthew 28:19-20 is a passage we reference often when discussing the responsibility of believers to evangelize and make disciples, and rightly so. However, in my opinion many speakers using this passage emphasize one word of verse 19 ("go") to the exclusion of the emphasis Jesus made when He declared, "Go therefore...." Jesus' point was that we should be making disciples wherever we go *because He is the Lord of lords to whom all authority has been given.* "All authority has been given to Me in heaven and on earth. Go therefore and make disciples of all the nations" (Matthew 28:18-20).

Jesus is not only Lord of creation in that He made everyone and everything. He is also Lord of redemption, the one who sacrificed Himself to die in the place of sinful men, taking the wages of sin upon Himself; the one who conquered sin and death by rising from the dead; the only one through whom a person can and must be delivered from sin (Acts 4:12).

This is the message shining forth in such wonderful passages as Acts 2:22-36, where Peter describes Jesus as the one whom God raised up and exalted to the place of authority on His right hand. Peter's conclusion is forceful, "Therefore let all the house of Israel know for certain that God has made Him both Lord and Christ—this Jesus whom you crucified" (Acts 2:36).

Consider also the declaration of Peter and his fellows to the Sanhedrin as they chose to obey God rather than men because, "The God of our fathers raised up Jesus, whom you had put to death by hanging Him on a cross. He is the one whom God exalted to His right hand as a Prince and a Savior, to grant repentance to Israel, and forgiveness of sins" (Acts 5:30-31). The apostles are boldly telling the Council, "We can't stop teaching in the name of Jesus! He's the Lord through whom God has granted salvation to Israel!"

The letters of Paul abound with the same message. As he opens his letter to the Roman believers, the apostle identifies himself as being set apart for the gospel of God which concerns

His Son "who was declared the Son of God with power by the resurrection from the dead...Jesus Christ our Lord" (Romans 1:4).

Praying for the Ephesians, Paul desires that they would know "the surpassing greatness of His power toward us who believe...in accordance with the working of the strength of His might which He brought about in Christ, when He raised Him from the dead and seated Him at His right hand in the heavenly *places*, far above all rule and authority and power and dominion, and every name that is named, not only in this age but also in the one to come. And He put all things in subjection under His feet, and gave Him as head over all things to the church" (Ephesians 1:19-22).

Having described the humiliation and death of Christ in obedience to the Father (Philippians 2:6-8), Paul goes on to announce, "For this reason also, God highly exalted Him, and bestowed on Him the name which is above every name, so that at the name of Jesus EVERY KNEE WILL BOW, of those who are in heaven and on earth and under the earth, and that every tongue will confess that Jesus Christ is Lord, to the glory of God the Father" (Philippians 2:9-11).

With this identification of Jesus Christ as the Lord of all by virtue of His resurrection and exaltation, we are not surprised to find Him telling His apostles that their mission is to testify of Him (Acts 1:8). Who else is worth telling about? Who else has accomplished what Jesus accomplished? Who else has been given all authority in heaven and on earth?

This is Jesus' whole point in Matthew 28:18-20. Because He is the Lord of the universe, making disciples for Him is not a burdensome chore placed upon unwilling messengers. It is the joyous privilege of those who have already recognized His greatness and want everyone else to magnify Him as He alone deserves. Evangelism is simply the activity of helping others see reality—the truth that Jesus Christ is Lord of all.

Because of the Biblical Pattern

Peter on Pentecost

When the Holy Spirit came upon the believers gathered in Jerusalem on the day of Pentecost and they started speaking in tongues to the diverse crowd of Jews assembled to observe the occasion, it is interesting to note what their audience heard. According to the testimony of the crowd, "we hear them in our own tongues speaking of the mighty deeds of God" (Acts 2:11).

As Peter spoke further to the multitude that day, there is a decided centrality of the person and work of God in Christ. God attested Jesus (Acts 2:22), planned His betrayal and death (2:23), raised Him from the dead and exalted Him to the right hand of the Father's throne (2:24-35). It was God who, by plan and performance, "made Him both Lord and Christ—this Jesus whom you crucified" (2:36).

Up to this point in Peter's message, all attention is on God. When the audience has been mentioned, it is only to point out their role in putting Jesus to death (2:23, 36)! Peter's theme has been who Jesus is and what God has done through Him.

What is the result of this theocentric approach? The crowd was overwhelmed with the magnitude of their crime against God, having rejected the very one whom God had made Lord and Messiah. Their question for the apostles was, "Brethren, what shall we do?" (2:37). It is at this juncture Peter calls them to repentance and identification with Jesus, looking to Him for forgiveness and the promised presence of the Holy Spirit (2:38-39).

Peter and John

This theocentric approach to evangelism is repeated consistently throughout the history of the early church given to us in the book of Acts. Ponder Peter's message at the portico of Solomon after the lame man was made able to walk (Acts 3:12-26). Consider his brief messages before the Sanhedrin while being tried for proclaiming Jesus (Acts 4:8-12; 5:29-32). They are all designed to make known the work of God in Christ, whose identity and ministry demand repentance on man's part and enable forgiveness of sins.

Stephen

Stephen's message to the Sanhedrin was God-centered in approach, even though it was designed to reproach his audience more than to evangelize. He goes to great lengths describing how God worked throughout Israel's history—calling and covenanting with Abraham (Acts 7:2-8), rescuing Joseph and making him a ruler in Egypt (7:9-16), sending Moses to deliver Israel from Egyptian slavery (7:20-43), driving out the Canaanites through Joshua (7:44-45), establishing His special presence in Solomon's temple (7:46-50) and sending His word through prophets to the nation throughout its history (7:51-53).

Even as God worked in these wonderful ways for His people, Stephen demonstrates throughout his message how the nation rejected Him. Israel's ancestors sold Joseph into slavery (7:9). The nation disowned Moses at first (7:35), disobeyed him as God's spokesman (7:38-39) and worshiped idols in front of him (7:40-43). Furthermore, they persecuted and often killed the prophets whom God in mercy sent to call His people back to Himself (7:51-52a).

The climax of Stephen's message is in Acts 7:52b-53. He charges the nation of Israel, through its leaders, with acting just like their rebellious forefathers who rejected God's prophets. Only now they had resisted the Holy Spirit by betraying and murdering God's Righteous One, the Messiah whom He had promised so frequently through the prophets.

Peter with Cornelius

Once more Peter is the messenger when the gospel is taken to the God-fearing gentile Cornelius with his friends and family in Caesarea. The apostle does not deviate from his policy of directing the attention to the person of God and His deliverance through Jesus of Nazareth. Reminding his hearers of the life and ministry of Jesus, Peter asserts that all He did was the result of God's anointing Him with the Holy Spirit and with power (Acts 10:36-38). When Jesus was crucified, God raised Him from the dead and appointed Him Judge of the living and the dead (10:39-42). It is through this Jesus that forgiveness of sin may be received (10:43).

Paul at Antioch

When Paul enters the picture as an apostolic messenger of the gospel, his God-centered approach is as evident as Peter's and Stephen's. His message in the synagogue at Antioch starts with a Bible history lesson, in which Paul reminds those present how God chose Abraham, delivered Israel out of Egypt, brought the nation into Canaan and provided judges and kings for the people (Acts 13:16-22).

In keeping with His promise, God then provided Israel a Savior, whom Paul identifies as Jesus (13:23-25). The salvation Jesus provides involved His death at the request of the Jews and His resurrection by the power of God (13:26-37).

Paul's conclusion in this message is that forgiveness of sins is available through Jesus and that freedom from sin is also available through Him (13:38-39). With that in mind, he warns the people not to reject in unbelief what God has done in Christ (13:40-41).

By now a recognizable pattern is emerging in the preaching and evangelism of the early church. The substance of every message is who God is and what He has done, culminating in the resurrection and exaltation of His Son, Jesus Christ. Any mention of man is in either of two closely-related contexts: his hardness of heart and sinful rebellion against God, or his need to repent and receive God's forgiveness.

Paul in Athens

Up to this point, all evangelistic messages recorded in Acts have been to Jews with a strong Old Testament background or to God-fearing gentiles such as Cornelius who also understood Old Testament history. What happens when the gospel is taken to the pagans, the heathen of the gentile world who knew nothing at all about God? Does the approach change? Is there any less emphasis on God?

Paul's speech to the philosophers at the Areopagus in Athens answers those questions forcefully. Finding introductory material in his observation of their altar to an unknown god among their other idols and objects of worship, the apostle proceeds to tell them about the God of whom they have no knowledge (Acts 17:22-23).

This God, Paul states, is the Creator of all things and Lord of heaven and earth (17:24). He depends on man in no way, but rather is the Provider of everything man needs to exist and thrive (17:25). His sovereignty is absolute and comprehensive, and He desires that man would seek Him to whom we owe our very existence (17:26-28). The thrust of the message so far is completely on who God is and what He has done!

Such a God cannot be represented by an image of precious metal or stone, asserts His messenger (17:29). This is a direct affront to and a strong rebuke of the altar the Athenians had made to the unknown god. Paul is clearly showing them that they could not hope to appease the true God by erecting an altar to Him. He deserved far more than that!

This God whom they had slighted for so many centuries in their ignorance is now calling for repentance on the part of all (17:30). This is no light matter, since judgment of the world is certain and will be carried out righteously by His appointed Judge, whom God validated to the world by raising Him from the dead (17:31).

That was as far as Paul got in his message, due to the sneers of some people in his audience. However, we have seen enough to know that the approach Paul used with these heathens is completely true to the pattern of theocentrism found earlier in Acts. His message was about God. Man's role in the picture is to see how he has dishonored God and to repent.

Paul before Agrippa

When Paul appeared before Agrippa as a prisoner of Rome, his defense consists of a testimony of how Jesus met him on the road to Damascus and commissioned him to evangelize the gentile world (Acts 26:2-18). However, what is significant for our purposes is the summary Paul gives of the evangelistic message he proclaimed in obedience to the Lord (26:19-23).

The apostle affirms, "So having obtained help from God, I stand to this day testifying both to small and great, stating nothing but what the Prophets and Moses said was going to take place; that the Christ was to suffer, *and* that by reason of *His* resurrection from the dead He would be the first to proclaim light both to the *Jewish* people and to the Gentiles" (26:22-23). Paul is stating clearly that his gospel was only "Jesus Christ, and Him crucified" (1 Corinthians 2:2). His message was completely theocentric, by design. And it is on the basis of this gospel that he called both Jews and gentiles to "repent and turn to God" (Acts 26:20).

If there is anything to be learned from a survey of New Testament evangelism, it is that the gospel consists of the person and work of God. It is solely on the basis of who He is and what He has done through God the Son, Jesus Christ, that we are to call people to repentance and faith in Him.

CHAPTER THREE

How to Evangelize Theocentrically

The formula for God-centered evangelism is not difficult to express. The challenge comes in the doing of it! As a strategy, theocentric evangelism consists of two activities.

God-centered Living

The starting point for theocentric evangelism is God-centered living! God-centered lives provide undeniable evidence of the truth of a God-centered gospel. On the other hand, nothing undermines the gospel more quickly or effectively than a messenger whose life denies the words that are spoken. The character of Talkative in *The Pilgrim's Progress* illustrates this well.

Consider the impact on this world of a person who knows and lives in light of the God who is enough. In a society filled with worry and fear, this person accepts life's circumstances with the calm assurance that God is in control and has a purpose in what is happening. In a culture always demanding more, this Christian demonstrates contentment with what God has provided, because He is the God who is enough.

In a dog-eat-dog environment, the God-centered believer treats others as he would want to be treated in the same situation (Matthew 7:12). In an atmosphere filled with people demanding their "rights," the theocentric child of God is secure enough in Him to sacrificially love the unloving.

This transformation into being God-centered in daily living is an ongoing process in our Christian lives. While it is the work of God, it is also our responsibility! "And do not be conformed to this world, but be transformed by the renewing of your mind, so that you may prove what the will of God is, that which is good and acceptable and perfect" (Romans 12:2). Here we are commanded to be transformed, yet the transformation itself is something done to us.[1]

The key to fulfilling our responsibility in this process is what we feed our minds. We become more theocentric as we meditate upon the perfections of our Sovereign Lord and the beauty of His holy character. As we fill ourselves with what He has revealed about Himself in His word, God's Spirit can use what we take in and ponder to transform us more and more into His image. What we think about plays a major role in what we become.

This being the case, focus your mind on the splendor of who God is and the marvels of what He has done and promises to do. Tear yourself away from the hours of entertainment provided by this world and fill yourself with material the Spirit of God can use to transform you to Christ-likeness. Those to whom you bear witness of the saving power of Jesus Christ will take note.

God-centered Proclamation

In addition to our God-centered daily living, theocentric evangelism also involves a God-centered presentation of Biblical truth. This aspect of evangelism also requires careful examination.

Think for a few moments about some of the familiar stories found in the Bible. Consider, for example, the accounts of Cain

---

[1] The words "be transformed" translate a present passive imperative form of μεταμορφόω.

and Abel (Genesis 4), the flood (Genesis 6-9), Babel (Genesis 11), the burning bush (Exodus 3-4) and the 10 commandments (Exodus 20). Or ponder the tabernacle of Israel, the conquest of Canaan, the killing of Goliath and the den of lions. When these narratives are preached or taught, what do most people remember about them?

Having asked this question many times of hundreds of people in every area of the country, I am still waiting to hear any Christian tell me that they think of God! Every answer to this point has evidenced that people remember either the details or the people of the Biblical stories.[2]

Of course, the details and the people of these stories are important. However, something is definitely wrong when we come away from looking at God's Word without being pointed primarily to His character and His work. Our attitude in teaching and preaching should be that people may remember some details and some people from these accounts, but they *must* remember God! The same principle holds for evangelism.

A theocentric approach to evangelism means that, when discussing events described in the Bible, we will stress how God used them to reveal and glorify Himself. For example, why did God send the plagues on Egypt? As we take unbelievers through our *Discovering God* Bible study, we show them the four reasons

---

[2] From a study of two hundred sermons found in *Pulpit Digest* and *Preaching* between 1981 and 1991, David F. Wells reports that "The overwhelming proportion of the sermons analyzed - more than 80 percent - were anthropocentric." He continues by observing, "It is as if God has become an awkward appendage to the practice of evangelical faith, at least as measured by the pulpit" (*No Place for Truth: or Whatever Happened to Evangelical Theology?* [Grand Rapids: William B. Eerdmans Publishing Company, 1993] pp. 251-252). This being the case, it is no wonder people leave the preaching services with their thoughts on man and details rather than God!

God gave for those plagues. In doing so, we emphasize that three of the four reasons have to do with God's glory directly! Then we go on to detail the plagues, highlighting how each plague is a direct confrontation with the gods of Egypt in which the God of Israel proves Himself infinitely superior.

When presenting the people of the Biblical narratives, a theocentric approach accentuates how God develops their character and uses their actions and attitudes to His own purposes. The issue is not so much that people "Dare to Be a Daniel" as that they have a clear understanding of the greatness of God who made Daniel the faithful boy and man he was! There is no such thing as a self-made Christian or a self-made godly person. It is God who works in us "both to will and to work for *His* good pleasure" (Philippians 2:13).

A theocentric presentation of the gospel will describe how the good news of Jesus Christ revolves around God's purpose of glorifying Himself. It will point out that the essence of sin is man's failure to fulfill the reason for his existence: to glorify God by enjoying His absolute and complete sufficiency. It will confront nonbelievers with the opportunity to repent and devote the remainder of their lives to delighting in the God who is enough!

When God is the sum and substance of evangelism, common appeals to nonbelievers by modern evangelicals fall by the wayside. The issue is no longer merely "fire escape," nor even going to heaven ("Where will you be five minutes after you die?"). Heaven without God would be hell! The single issue of theocentric evangelism is God, the reality of who He is and the opportunity of knowing Him whom to know is life eternal.

Responsibilities God places on people are always based on the character of God in a theocentric approach to evangelism. The 10 Commandments are not presented merely as a list of "Thou shalts" and "Thou shalt nots" which must be obeyed in order to avoid punishment or enjoy blessing. True, they were given to Israel in "Thou shalt" and "Thou shalt not" form. It is also true that disobedience brought severe punishment and obedience guaranteed delightful blessings.

However, the common mistake in teaching the 10 Commandments is that we often start in Exodus 20:3, when we should begin with and underscore Exodus 20:1-2! Exodus 20:3-17 mean nothing until we realize that they are based by God Himself on who He is ("I am the LORD your God") and what He has done ("who brought you out of the land of Egypt, out of the house of slavery"). The 10 Commandments were a means God provided for Israel to live in light of who He is and what He had done for them. The fact that Israel could not keep the 10 Commandments or any other elements of the Law was clear evidence of the devastating depravity of sin.

When this theocentric approach to the 10 Commandments is taken with nonbelievers, important groundwork is laid for those who do trust Christ. As new Christians, they will already have a foundation for understanding that God's character is the basis for all that Christians should be and do. We are to love because He is love (1 John 4:10-11). We are to endure undeserved suffering at the hands of others because our Lord did the same (1 Peter 2:21-23). We are to avoid murdering because God's image is in every person (Genesis 9:6). We are to be holy because our God is holy (Leviticus 19:2; 1 Peter 1:15-16).

It is safe to say that God never gives a command that is not based on His character. Realizing this will go a long way in preventing legalism, for obedience becomes an issue of glorifying Him by reflecting His character. One intended result of theocentric evangelism is Christians whose primary motivation for obedience is God's holy character and what He has done for us, rather than guilt or fear of punishment.

Finally, the theocentric approach will connect the *how* of our responsibilities with God's character, as well as the *why*. No, Israel couldn't keep the 10 Commandments. Neither can any natural person today, apart from the miracle of the new birth which God alone brings about through the work of the Holy Spirit. Living in light of who God is and what He has done is impossible—until God transforms and empowers us. This is the beauty of God's promise to Israel through his prophet Ezekiel, "I will put My Spirit within you and cause you to walk in My statues, and you will be careful to observe My ordinances" (Ezekiel 36:27).

The Christian life operates on the same principle. We do not become what God wants or obey what God commands by trying harder or doing more. It is the faithfulness of God working in us to will and do His good pleasure that brings about faithful, godly living. We simply trust Him, living by faith in Him the same way as did those men and women of old (Hebrews 10:35-11:40).

God's trustworthy character is the key to the Christian life of faith, nothing else. And how we evangelize nonbelievers will lay the groundwork for how they understand the Christian life as believers. We must lay that groundwork theocentrically.

PART TWO

CHRONOLOGICAL BIBLE STUDY

CHAPTER FOUR

What is Evangelistic Chronological Bible Study?

Whether ministering to one person, one couple or a living room full of nonbelievers, the method of evangelism I recommend whenever possible is chronological Bible study. Starting with creation and proceeding in chronological order, open the Scriptures to these people and show them how God's character and gracious outworking of redemption are revealed in the narratives of His Word. Trace His promises of a Redeemer over time through the Old Testament, until Jesus Christ is revealed as the complete fulfillment of those commitments.

This does not mean every event and every passage in Scripture must be covered. Most are not. In the *Discovering God* Bible study we have 24 sessions.[1] There is no way we can discuss in detail every story and passage of the Bible in only 24 sessions!

Our agenda in an evangelistic chronological Bible study is two-fold: 1) to allow God to reveal Himself through the Biblical accounts which are discussed, and 2) to trace His plan of redemption from Genesis 3:15 until it is fulfilled in the resurrected and exalted Lord, Jesus Christ. These purposes govern the selection of passages we study as well as the manner in which we study them.

---

[1] See Appendix A for the table of contents of *Discovering God*, the chronological Bible study developed in my own evangelistic ministry as a pastor. More information on how to obtain *Discovering God* study materials is found in the back of this book.

APPENDIX A

Discovering God Table of Contents

Acknowledgements
Introduction
Effective Use of *Discovering God*
Glossary
Introductory Matters
Lesson 1 - The God of Creation: The Spirit World
Lesson 2 - The God of Creation: The Material Universe (Part 1)
Lesson 3 - The God of Creation: The Material Universe (Part 2)
Lesson 4 - Man's Separation from God
Lesson 5 - God Deals with Cain and Abel
Lesson 6 - The God of the Flood
Lesson 7 - God and Babel
Lesson 8 - The God of Abram
Lesson 9 - The God Who Is Enough
Lesson 10 - The God of Isaac
Lesson 11 - The God of Joseph
Lesson 12 - The God of Moses
Lesson 13 - God and the Plagues of Egypt
Lesson 14 - The God of Passover
Lesson 15 - The God of the 10 Commandments
Lesson 16 - The God of the Tabernacle
Lesson 17 - Israel's God from Moses to Malachi
Lesson 18 - Immanuel—God With Us

Lesson 19 - Jesus' Baptism and Testing
Lesson 20 - The God of the New Birth
Lesson 21 - The Seed and the Soil
Lesson 22 - Jesus—the Great I AM
Lesson 23 - Jesus' Passion and Death
Lesson 24 - Jesus—Exalted Lord
Summary from God's Perspective

CHAPTER FIVE

Why is Chronological Bible Study Needed in Evangelism?

Three categories must be considered in developing the urgent need to make chronological Bible study a basic evangelistic approach in our ministry. First, we will investigate three Biblical reasons. Then we will take a look at the society in which we live, to see how its characteristics call for a chronological approach. Finally, we will see how the chronological Bible study approach is called for in light of a basic principle of ministry modeled in the personal evangelism of Jesus Christ Himself.

Biblical Reasons

The Way God Worked

Contemplate the opening words of the letter to the Hebrews for a few moments: "God, after He spoke long ago to the fathers in the prophets in many portions and in many ways, in these last days has spoken to us in His Son, whom He appointed heir of all things, through whom also He made the world" (Hebrews 1:1-2).

When I read this passage, a question jumps to my mind: Why didn't God just speak through His Son from the beginning? After all, Hebrews makes it abundantly clear that the Son is vastly superior to the prophets, the angels, Moses, the Levitical priesthood and anyone else we might consider in this world. So why not just start with the best and stick with it?

There is a reason, of course. The all-wise God knew what He was doing! He even condescends to share some of His thinking about this approach with us, which we find in Galatians 4:4. In terms of what Paul wrote to the Galatians, God chose not to speak through His Son until 2,000 years ago because it wasn't time yet! There was so much that needed to happen first. So much background preparation had to be finished. Mankind needed to fully experience bondage under the elemental things of the world. The context for the gospel had not yet been completed. "But when the fullness of the time came, God sent forth His Son...."

All of which leads to another question: If God took thousands of years to set the context for the gospel before fulfilling it in Jesus Christ, why do we think people today will grasp the gospel apart from its context? How can we expect them to truly understand or appreciate the work of Christ when they have no idea who God is, what sin is, how sin has devastated human life, the concept of substitutionary atonement or the marvelous promises of a Redeemer which God repeated constantly throughout the Old Testament?

Biblical faith has never been a leap in the dark. Biblical faith is man's response to God's revelation of who He is and what He has done. Biblical faith is based on facts. Biblical faith is a response to truth. "So faith *comes* from hearing, and hearing by the word of Christ" (Romans 10:17). We cannot evoke faith in a nonbeliever—that is the work of the Holy Spirit. However, we can give that nonbeliever the context of truths about God, sin, atonement and promises of redemption. In fact, that is our privilege and responsibility.

One further question: Does it not make sense that the most

helpful way to present the gospel in context is to set forth its context the same way God did—chronologically?

The Example of Christ

Picture Cleopas and his companion as they shuffled down the path to Emmaus, shattered by the events of the past week. They had thought that Jesus the Nazarene was the hope of Israel, but three days earlier He had been crucified by the leaders of the nation. Now, they didn't even know where His body could be found, for it had disappeared from the tomb where it had been placed.

Now this Stranger meets them and walks with them, listening to their tale of woe. But rather than giving them His shoulders as crying pads, He chides them, "O foolish men and slow of heart to believe in all that the prophets have spoken! Was it not necessary for the Christ to suffer these things and to enter into His glory?" (Luke 24:25-26).

What happens next is significant. "Then beginning with Moses and with all the prophets, He explained to them the things concerning Himself in all the Scriptures" (Luke 24:27). Jesus gave these men the context for the gospel, starting with Moses (the Pentateuch—Genesis through Deuteronomy) and proceeding through the prophetic Scriptures. Our Lord used the chronological approach the first time the gospel of Jesus Christ was ever presented after His resurrection! And He did it with men who were already counted among His disciples, who had frequently heard Him teach during the months before this encounter.

If laying the context for the gospel chronologically was the approach Christ took with men who were raised with a strong Old Testament background as devout Jews and had been following Him for some time, how much more essential is it that we follow this same procedure with people who have no background at all?

The Design of the Bible

Jesus told His antagonistic Jewish listeners, "You search the Scriptures because you think that in them you have eternal life; it is these that testify about Me" (John 5:39). He was obviously referring to what we call the Old Testament Scriptures, telling His audience to learn about Him there even though He was in their presence at the time!

If people are to truly understand and appreciate who Jesus is, they must first be grounded in the Old Testament. He must be seen in the context of eternity and history.

The gospel writers, moved by the Holy Spirit, certainly understood that fact. Notice how each of them presents his account of the earthly life and ministry of the Christ by including the historical context.

Matthew, seeking to present Jesus as God's Messiah, places Him in context by tracing His genealogy from Abraham (Matthew 1:1-2). Immediately he has taken his readers back to Genesis 11:27 and made it clear that we must view Jesus in the context of Old Testament history.

Mark (1:2-3) starts his account of the life of Jesus Christ with quotations from Malachi 3:1 and Isaiah 40:3. The message in his approach is that our understanding of Jesus must develop, at least in part, from the prophetic portions of God's Word.

Luke takes his readers back even farther. When he sets forth the genealogy of Jesus, it is developed all the way to creation, ending with "Adam, the son of God" (Luke 3:38). This is an essential approach for his readers to recognize Jesus as the Son of man.

However, it is John who takes us back even before creation and places Jesus in the context of eternity. Opening his gospel with the words "In the beginning was the Word" (1:1), John makes it clear that if we are to know Jesus as we ought, we must see Him in light of His pre-existence as God. This is reinforced with a reference to Jesus as the Creator (John 1:3), indicating that we must go back to creation if we are to begin understanding Jesus in a historical context.

Each of the gospels also contains abundant quotations, references and allusions to the Old Testament throughout the narrative of Christ's life. This should also alert us to the importance of the larger historical context in enabling people to understand who Jesus is. We can safely assert that the gospel accounts are based upon Old Testament truth and cannot be properly understood apart from their Old Testament context.

Societal Reasons

If the United States of America ever was a "Christian" nation, it certainly is not now. We are what I call a "post-Christian society," in which the great majority of the population is Biblically illiterate and largely unchurched.[1] What this means is that people do not have a context for understanding the gospel. For effective outreach in this post-Christian generation, it is imperative that we give people this context for understanding the precious good news of life found in Jesus Christ.

It is not enough for us to give people the facts of the gospel—

---

[1] For example, a study of church attendance in America estimates that 20% of professing Protestants and 28% of professing Catholics are in church on any given weekend. C. Kirk Hadaway, Penny Long Marler and Mark Chaves, "What the Polls Don't Show: A Closer Look at U.S. Church Attendance," *American Sociological Review*, December, 1993, pp. 741-752. This, of course, does not take into account the 30% of our population 18 and older that are "totally secular in outlook." Kenneth L. Woodward, "The Rites of Americans," *Newsweek*, November 29, 1993, p. 82.

its details. You may tell a person he is a sinner and condemned but that God in love sent His Son Jesus to die for sinners. You can recount that Jesus rose from the dead and proclaim to your listener that he can be saved from sin by trusting in Him. Those are the details of the gospel. To us they are priceless truths. However, to someone without a context for understanding these facts, they are nothing but confusion.

Consider how most nonbelievers hear those details of the gospel. How much do they grasp its meaning? Do they know what sin is *Biblically*, rather than sociologically or psychologically? Do they understand what condemnation involves (it is more than future existence in the lake of fire)? Who do they understand Jesus to be? For that matter, when we talk about God, whom do they have in mind? How could Jesus die in my place 2,000 years ago, before I ever existed? What does it mean to trust Christ?

If nonbelievers are going to understand those details, we must take the time to present the gospel *in its Biblical context*. We must stop making assumptions about our listeners that lead us to shortchange them as we share the gospel with them.

We Cannot Assume People Know Anything about God

We live in a day and a culture in which many people know nothing at all about God. Their familiarity with Him is nothing beyond taking His name in vain during conversations. Even many churched people "know" a god who doesn't exist. Their concepts of God frequently are affected by New Age ideas and other perversions of truth. Yes, even some who sit in the pews of evangelical churches define God according to what they want Him to be and how they want Him to act.

The desperate need of our culture and our world is to know who God is as He has revealed Himself in His Word. This is an understanding that is most effectively gained through investigating His words and actions in the historical narratives of the Bible—the stories! It is in those passages where His character comes to life for people. It is in those passages where they see how His character impacts them most forcefully.

Take Pete, who attended one of our *Discovering God* studies from beginning to end. One evening after the study time was over, he didn't leave the living room to enjoy socializing and dessert in the kitchen. He just sat in his chair with hands folded, staring at the floor. Knowing that something was going on with him, I stayed in my chair nearby, waiting for Pete to verbalize whatever was on his mind. Finally he raised his head and quietly commented, "Boy, God sure expects a commitment, doesn't He!"

What is most interesting about Pete's remark is that the subject of commitment was never discussed that evening. It was not an element of the lesson or the Scripture we were covering. However, what Pete had been learning about God in previous sessions, combined with what he learned about God that night had made him realize that God is God, and as God He has every right to our undivided love, loyalty and obedience. The cumulative effect of the sessions in which he saw God revealing Himself chronologically through the events of the Bible was a powerful factor in Pete's understanding who God is and what that meant for him.

We Cannot Assume People Understand Our Terminology

Even beyond what was mentioned earlier about the way nonbelievers hear the details of the gospel, we must be concerned with the terms we use when presenting the gospel. We throw key words at our hearers without considering that they do not understand what we mean by them.

Salvation

The words *saved* and *salvation* are good examples. When I

served in youth evangelism, I conversed with a young man brought to me by a frustrated counselor. In the course of our conversation, I asked him if he had been saved. He answered, "Yes," so I followed that up by asking him to tell me about it. The lad proceeded to describe how he had fallen from a galloping horse and escaped injury!

Had he been "saved?" Yes! Was I glad for him? Undeniably! However, further conversation made it clear this youth had no concept of what it meant to be delivered from the penalty, power and presence of sin through the finished work of Jesus Christ. It was my responsibility to help him understand the term *saved* as it applied to his spiritual condition.

Grace

Sure, almost everyone in America has heard the song "Amazing Grace" sung at one time or another. Perhaps at a funeral or in a movie, or maybe in church. But that doesn't mean they know what *grace* means from a Biblical perspective. Some people think of *grace* as a word describing the smooth movements of a professional ice skater or the proper manners of an experienced hostess. A religious person might even relate the term to a brief prayer uttered before a meal.

Few are aware that the grace of God is His unmerited love and favor toward man. Because they don't understand the devastation of sin, they cannot comprehend the magnitude of God's grace. Their minds are so filled with concepts such as "my rights" and "justice" and "I'm worth it" that Biblical grace is completely foreign to their thinking.

Faith

My first week as a pastor I visited a home in which a woman told us, "Oh, I have a lot of faith."

"That's wonderful!" I replied. "Tell us, what is faith?"

After looking at us for a while as she thought it over, her response was, "I don't know." And she had been in church most of her life! What a joy it was to share with her Biblical passages that helped her see what *God, sin, condemnation, Jesus Christ, grace, faith* and *salvation* were really all about! An even greater privilege was seeing her confess with her mouth the Lord, Jesus Christ, coming to know personally as well as mentally what those truths mean.

Holiness

At one *Discovering God* session in which the holiness of God was a key topic, Judy leaned back against the fireplace and exclaimed, "I always thought God's holiness was His goodness and kindness!" She had also been in church most of her life. But learning what *holy* meant that evening was a key moment for her. Until she understood *holiness*, she did not understand accurately who God is.

Some Christians frustrate nonbelievers to an unbelievable extreme by using terms like *justification, redemption, sanctification* and *covenant*, rattling them off with no attempt to define them. And we tend to speak in such a condescending manner that those we evangelize are uncomfortable about asking what the words mean. So they nod and agree and sometimes even pray a prayer when invited, all the time thinking, "Anything to get rid of this guy! What in the world is he talking about?"

The point is that defining our terms is essential to providing a genuine understanding of God and His gospel. It is part of giving people a context for that understanding. And the best way I have found to define these terms is in the settings of the historical narratives of the Bible taken in chronological order. When this approach is used, the terms relate to real people and real life situations. The concepts of the terms involved are readily understandable by nonbelievers when viewed in these settings. And the impact of what they learn about God builds more and more by viewing these narratives in chronological order.

Try and put yourself in Steve's place for a moment. He attended a *Discovering God* study from the beginning. So he first learned about God's greatness and sovereign power in creation. Then he saw God's purity as we looked at the Fall, followed by His justice and grace in the Flood. After tracing the providence of God in the lives of Abraham, Isaac and Jacob, a taste of deliverance and redemption was provided Steve through looking at the Exodus from Egypt.

Then we looked at the tabernacle, that wonderful object lesson for teaching the holiness of God. It is such a clear picture of how God, who deigns to dwell in the midst of His nation, is still completely set apart from them because of His purity and their sinfulness. So we spend considerable time showing how God buffered Himself from the nation through the curtains and courtyards and layout of the tabernacle and camp of Israel.

This lesson closes with a discussion of the burnt offering, which reinforces the fact of man's sinfulness separating him from God. So we detail how the Israelite brought his sheep to the courtyard and pressed his hand on the sheep's head, symbolically identifying himself with the animal as his substitute and "transferring" his sin to the animal. Then we relate how the sheep's throat is cut, the blood caught and splattered on the altar, the carcass cut up and burned completely on the altar.

One principle we conclude from our study of the burnt offering is that sin's penalty is death, either the death of the sinner or the death of a substitute. A second principle is that, if the substitute sacrifice is acceptable to God, the sinner becomes acceptable to God.

When I ended the session after discussing these principles that evening, I said, "Okay, I'm done."

Steve jumped from his chair in the back of the room and waved his arms above his head shouting, "Hold it! You can't stop now! I don't have a sheep!"

He was dead serious. Why? Because the cumulative impact of everything he had learned about God, sin and himself through this chronological approach made him keenly aware of the issues involved. He saw his desperate need of a substitute sacrifice, and here we were ending the study for that evening! When we told Steve privately about the Lamb of God who had been sacrificed at Calvary, there was no confusion in his mind about what that meant or what he needed to do about it. His response was a direct result of God working in his mind and heart by means of the theocentric, chronological Bible study.

We Cannot Assume People Consciously Accept and Appreciate Absolutes

In fact, in our post-modern society we can often safely assume that the people to whom we are talking no longer recognize any absolutes. With many Americans, everything is relative, including truth, morality, ethics and authority.

This failure to recognize absolutes affects how they hear what we are saying when we share the truths of the gospel of God with them. We cannot expect people to believe what we tell them simply because the Bible says it. They don't think that way! They are unconvinced that the Bible is God's Word. And even if it is, that doesn't make much difference to them because God Himself is viewed as relative in our culture.

God's perfect holiness and purity are difficult to accept for people who do not think in terms of absolutes. His infinite power, wisdom and knowledge are hard to embrace, not only because of unbelief but also because they are not accustomed to thinking in terms of absolutes about anything or anyone.

What does this mean for us as we seek to reach out to our society with the glorious gospel of God? Two matters come quickly to mind. First, this should drive us to our knees in fervent prayer for those to whom we minister. It does no good for us to argue with them about the validity of absolutes and the lack of logic in their belief that everything is relative. The real, foundational issues involved are spiritual, not logical or philosophical. It takes the work of the Holy Spirit in the hearts of nonbelievers revealing the God of eternity in all His splendor and majesty. When their spiritual eyes are opened to see the God who is, they have no problems with absolutes anymore. They have encountered the Absolute.

Secondly, this cultural rejection of absolutes underscores the need for a chronological approach to evangelistic Bible study. I have watched time after time as people have entered our *Discovering God* Bible studies as skeptics with a relativist perspective on everything. We never confront their relativism directly. We just look at God as He reveals Himself in the narratives of Scripture. Before we are through the 24-session course, these people are speaking in terms of absolutes as they discuss God and the issues that relate to Him. When they listen to themselves talk, they can't believe what they are saying!

What happened to them? The Holy Spirit wielded His sword in their hearts week after week as we spent time in the Word looking at who God is as He speaks and acts in those stories. Gradually their fear of absolutism is dispelled, as they see that God consistently proves Himself absolutely trustworthy, totally wise, completely righteous and infinitely powerful. Most people reject absolutism out of a fear of being disappointed, not because of a philosophical conviction. As they learn who God is, many of these beloved nonbelievers begin to realize the truth of Romans 10:11, "WHOEVER BELIEVES IN HIM WILL NOT BE DISAPPOINTED."

A Ministry Reason

The First Beatitude and Evangelism

The first blessing Jesus pronounced in His sermon on the mount was on those who are "poor in spirit" (Matthew 5:3). The nature of their blessing is that these poverty-stricken people are citizens of the kingdom of God!

Who are these whom Jesus describes as poor in spirit? They are those who recognize their complete spiritual destitution apart from God.[2] They realize their total unworthiness and inability in God's sight. As they kneel before God, they do so without pretense and with keen awareness that He is their only hope.

The poor in spirit are those like the tax collector who exclaimed, "God, be merciful to me, the sinner!" (Luke 18:13). He realized his absolute lack of righteousness before God and the fact that all he deserved was condemnation as a sinner. He pled with God to show him mercy by not treating him as he deserved. And it was this man rather than the self-righteous Pharisee who went home justified that day.

The lesson in both Matthew 5:3 and Luke 18:9-14 is essentially the same. God cannot declare righteous anyone who retains even a semblance of self-righteousness. His mercy and grace are given to those who see themselves spiritually destitute, mourn their condition and humbly turn to Him in faith as sinners starving

---

[2] D. A. Carson, "Matthew," ed. by Frank E. Gaebelein, *The Expositor's Bible Commentary*, vol. 8 (Grand Rapids, MI: The Zondervan Corporation, 1984), p. 132.

for true righteousness (Matthew 5:4-6). They are the ones who enjoy the blessings of His kingdom.

With this background, we do well to notice how Jesus ministered to Nicodemus. This man was the religious teacher of Israel and a member of the ruling Sanhedrin (John 3:1, 9). It was a foregone conclusion that if anyone in Israel had access to the kingdom of God, Nicodemus would be that person.

Precisely because Nicodemus and his peers viewed themselves that way, Jesus' first words to this man were, "Truly, truly, I say to you, unless one is born again he cannot see the kingdom of God" (John 3:3). Nicodemus needed to recognize his spiritual poverty, that he had nothing in himself qualifying him for entrance into God's kingdom. Until he was completely emptied of self-righteousness and relied totally on God's cleansing, regeneration by the Spirit and salvation through the Son, he stood condemned (John 3:5-8, 18-20).

The same principle held true in Jesus' ministry to the woman of Sychar, although the details of her situation certainly differed from those of Nicodemus. This woman was a Samaritan with no hope of achieving the status he had attained. No doubt her sense of self-satisfaction in life was a small fraction of what the teacher of Israel felt. She seems to be a perfect candidate for a "God loves you so come to Him" message.

Instead, Jesus tells her to go back to Sychar, get her husband and bring him back with her to meet Jesus at the well (John 4:16). Her brief reply is that she has no husband to bring (4:17). Then Jesus reveals awareness that the woman has had five husbands and is currently living in an immoral relationship with a man to whom she is not married (4:17-18).

Why did He do this? Why bring up the subject of her husband (or lack thereof) in the middle of a discussion about water springing up to eternal life (cf. 4:14)—especially when she had indicated her desire for such water (4:15)?

These questions become even more intense and appropriate when we remember that the woman's desire for this water was based on her misconception that Jesus was speaking about physical water. Jesus could have responded to her by simply pointing out that He was talking about something far greater, a satisfying of spiritual thirst. But He didn't.

Jesus brought up the subject of this woman's husband in order to confront her with her spiritual bankruptcy. Her immoral lifestyle reflected the destitution of her soul, and until she saw herself as she really was there was no reason to think she was ready for the solution to her need. Only those who know they are sick have any interest in medicine or surgery.

While there was still a semblance of self-righteousness in this woman's life, she would not thirst for God's righteousness. And until she thirsted for His righteousness, she would never be satisfied.

This principle provides strong support for taking a chronological Bible study approach to evangelism. When we take nonbelievers to the Old Testament and show them the glorious character of God revealed there, we provide for them the only Person with whom they should rightfully compare themselves. And when they make that comparison honestly as the Holy Spirit applies truth to their hearts, they realize their spiritual poverty and truly become poor in spirit. As we come to the Ten Commandments and show how they reflect the holy character of God, the fact of their spiritual destitution becomes even more painful to these dear nonbelievers.

Meanwhile, we continue to show them God's promises of a Redeemer who will come to deal with sin and the spiritual bankruptcy it causes. We also portray the rebelliousness and sin of Israel throughout the Old Testament. Nonbelievers can easily relate with that nation, and as they do the reality of their own sin becomes an even greater burden on their heart.

As the Spirit of God wields the sword of His Word in these hearts during a chronological Bible study, their sin becomes more than a fact. It becomes a personal, horrible reality. They become overwhelmed with the realization of their own depravity and cry out in despair when they don't have a sheep to make atonement! That's when we know the kingdom of heaven is theirs.

CHAPTER SIX

What to Expect when Studying the Bible Chronologically in Evangelism

When the Bible is studied from a theocentric, chronological perspective for evangelism purposes, we do so purposefully looking for specific results. When I am leading such a study, I have two major intended results in mind.

First, *I want the people attending to know the gospel in its context*. Whether they accept it and trust Christ is completely out of my control. However, as long as they are attending, I have the opportunity and the privilege of leading them to understand what the gospel is all about. As I lead the discussions and our team ministers to the people, I expect this to be accomplished.

In other words, these people will comprehend who God is, in keeping with what He has revealed about Himself in the Bible. They will know what sin is from His perspective, rather than from a psychological or sociological vantage point. They will understand the terms involved with the gospel, such as *holy, grace, truth, redeem*, etc. They will grasp who Jesus is and how in Him all the redemptive promises of God are fulfilled.

Secondly, I want the people who trust Christ while attending our evangelistic study to be so excited about God that they would never think of asking a church leader or Sunday school teacher to evangelize their friends, neighbors, fellow workers and relatives. *I want them to be so filled with wonder and awe at God's glory that they desire to share His greatness with everyone themselves.*

This can happen, when we take the time to open His Word and let Him reveal that glory to them through a theocentric, chronological Bible study. I know, because I've watched it take place.

PART THREE

USING THEOCENTRIC CHRONOLOGICAL BIBLE STUDIES IN EVANGELISM

CHAPTER SEVEN

Prayerfully Preparing

So here you are, realizing God has placed you in your neighborhood as a lighthouse to warn those living around you of the wages of sin and to illumine the way to God through Christ. You see the necessity of evangelizing theocentrically and the value of doing so using a chronological Bible study with your neighbors. What to do now?

Our experiences in conducting evangelistic chronological Bible studies have taught us much about how to organize, operate and follow up on these studies. In this section I will share some of what we have learned in hopes of providing a frame of reference for you to begin your own ministry. It will be the beginning of an adventure you will never forget!

The strategy presented here develops an outreach ministry to a neighborhood group. However, do not assume you have to gather a group of 15-20 nonbelievers before you can have a chronological Bible study in your neighborhood. When I started conducting evangelistic chronological Bible studies, it was with two people: a husband and wife in their home. Many are using these studies one-on-one with great impact, meeting with a neighbor over coffee or getting together every week with a friend or relative.

What follows is a strategy we have developed in ministering the gospel to adults in neighborhoods. If you are using the studies in different venues (teenagers, campus ministry, jail ministry, with fellow workers during lunch breaks, etc.), you will need to make adjustments. However, those adjustments should be fairly obvious as you consider your situation, and the basic principles of ministry will remain the same.

Prayerfully Preparing

Everything begins with *prayer*. We must remember at all times that we are merely tools. It is our privilege and a demonstration of the grace of God that He uses us to minister the message of His deliverance from sin through Christ to those around us (1 Timothy 1:12-14). We do not accomplish anything worthwhile for God. If something of eternal value is achieved, it will be because God has done it through us. "So then neither the one who plants nor the one who waters is anything, but God who causes the growth" (1 Corinthians 3:7).

Realizing these truths will drive us to "pray without ceasing" (1 Thessalonians 5:17). We need to pray for ourselves, because we are completely inadequate for the task at hand. We must pray for our nonbelieving neighbors, because they are dead in sin. We have to throw ourselves at the feet of God, extolling His mercy, grace, truth, righteousness, wrath, justice and love. Thank Him for revealing Himself and giving the opportunity of sharing the beauties of His holiness with others. Plead that He would make us bold, faithful messengers and that the Holy Spirit would open the blind eyes and soften the hard hearts to which we will minister.

The other ongoing element of preparation is *relationship building*, developing and deepening personal relationships with your neighbors. Effective ministry normally flows through meaningful relationships. It will be the relationships that have been established with your neighbors, friends and fellow workers which will provide the opportunity and the basis for ministering to them.

Make no mistake about it. Building relationships takes time and effort. There are no shortcuts. Take Jim and Bev, for example. They were hosts for one of the neighborhood chronological Bible studies I led, but the story of that neighborhood ministry started years before the study was held.

Jim and Bev moved into their neighborhood about five years before the study began. They were committed Christians with a heart for God and for the lost. Therefore, they purposed together before God to impact their neighborhood for Him. The first step, they realized, was getting to know these neighbors and letting the neighbors get to know them. So they looked for ways to get involved.

What they found out is that some of the neighbors got together weekly to go bowling. The bowling activity was on Friday nights starting at 10 o'clock. Now you need to understand a few things about this husband and wife at this point. First, they did not particularly like to bowl. Second, they were a young couple with three young children—one a newborn baby. Third, as with most people, Friday night was the end of the work week. They were exhausted.

In spite of these factors, Jim and Bev went bowling with their neighbors regularly. Of course, friendships started and other activities and events became part of their schedule in the neighborhood. Relationships deepened to the point where the group eventually asked this couple for help in finding something that would guide them in their marriages. So the group watched some videos giving advice for married people based on Biblical principles.

By this time, the neighbors trusted Jim and Bev. When they were invited into the family's home for a *Discovering God* study, they came. We averaged 20-25 adults meeting together for each session. God worked powerfully in their lives as we discussed His Word, and He has continued to do so since. It all started with a prayerful commitment to building relationships for the sake of the gospel of God on the part of one Christian couple.

Relationships are invaluable in ministry. They multiply the effectiveness of our ministry many times over. If you need evidence of that, just consider those whom God has used in your life to evangelize and disciple you. Notice the relationships that were involved, whether family or friend. So remember this: as difficult and time-consuming as it is to build relationships with your neighbors, it is worth it for the sake of the gospel.

CHAPTER EIGHT

Prayerfully Teaming

Team ministry was the norm in the New Testament. Jesus had a team (Mark 3:13-19) and sent out teams (Mark 6:7; Luke 10:1). His apostles followed the same method of operation, starting with Pentecost (Acts 2:14) and consistently throughout the early years of the church (Peter and John - Acts 3-4; Peter with fellow Christians from Joppa - Acts 10:23; Barnabas and Saul - Acts 11:25-26, 30; 13:1, 3; Barnabas and Mark - Acts 15:39; Paul and Silas - Acts 15:40).

The benefits of team ministry are manifold. One is that team ministry allows the exercise of a greater variety of spiritual gifts than is possible when going it alone. God has seen fit not to give any one person all the gifts needed for—or all the responsibility involved in—ministry. He designed us so we need each other if we are going to be most effective!

Another advantage of team ministry is the encouragement and help that team members can provide for one another. Because ministry involves people working with people, there are times of discouragement, exhaustion, inability, frustration and failure. In such moments the support, counsel and comfort of ministry partners become priceless.

There are also occasions when we tend to give ourselves credit for God's work, to view people as prospective "notches on our gun" or we seek to become the main attraction instead of giving God His rightful place. The value of team members who are willing to put us in our place at such times is immeasurable.

Especially when we are involved in reaching out to the nonbelieving world, team ministry is vitally important for an additional reason. As the team works together, it becomes a window for the world to see how Christians love each other. After all, that is the criterion that will decide for people whether or not we are truly disciples of Jesus Christ (John 13:35).

So unless you are ministering one-on-one with a neighbor, fellow worker or friend, you want to have a team. Therefore, the next step in the process is prayerfully putting together a ministry team that will serve those neighbors who come to the evangelistic chronological Bible study.

First and foremost, team members must be believers who know and love God, find their sufficiency in Him and want to make His glory known. They may be hesitant, but they must be willing to step forward for the cause of God's kingdom and the sake of His name.

Every individual on the team should understand the nature and importance of approaching evangelism theocentrically. They also need to grasp the purpose and value of a chronological approach to studying the Scriptures with nonbelievers. The whole team needs to be on the same page in these matters. The last thing you want is confusion, disorientation and division developing on the ministry team as the studies progress. There will be enough spiritual warfare going on without those problems!

Ideally, the team will involve other believers who are in the same neighborhood and have built relationships with many of the same people. This is not necessarily a requirement to be on the team, but it certainly increases the effectiveness of the ministry! What should be a requirement is that the team members live within reasonable proximity to the neighborhood in which the studies will be held. They need to be close enough to develop relationships with the people outside the study times themselves, near enough to be available in times of crisis, trauma or jubilation in the lives of the people.

Another consideration in forming a team is giftedness and ability. A variety of gifts and abilities should be represented on the team to see the highest degree of effectiveness. Some are essential, others are important and still more are icing on the cake. However, no two teams will ever represent the same mix of gifts.

Among the essential gifts and qualities needed on a team, I would include *teaching* and *hospitality*. Understanding, living and communicating truth is what characterizes a person who is able to teach. Someone should be able to open God's Word with the nonbelievers and discuss the stories and principles found there in a way which helps them understand what God is saying.

At the same time, these people must be made to feel welcome and comfortable, so they will be able to concentrate on the truth as it is presented and discussed. The atmosphere of a neighborhood study session is dependent to a great degree on the hospitality demonstrated by the hosts and the ministry team. As we will see later, food and social times are key components of showing hospitality.

The gift of *faith* is of huge importance. Let's be honest, not every nonbeliever comes to these studies with an open mind and heart. Some people attend with the intention of arguing against everything that is said, planning to disprove the Bible and exalt man to God's rightful place. How do we deal with them? By prayerfully exercising the gift of faith.

One woman came to our *Discovering God* sessions determined to debate almost everything the Bible said. She looked up all the information she could find in books, periodicals and over the internet, so she could use it to refute what God's Word taught. The first few sessions became so tense because of her attitude and vocal objections that our hosts became extremely nervous, wondering if we should even continue the studies.

Our response as a team was to calm the hosts by reminding them that God was in control of the situation and that He could deal with this woman as He saw fit. We discussed our responsibility as being twofold. First, we needed to faithfully pray in faith. Second, we needed to let the Spirit of God control our thoughts, attitudes, words and actions, so that we would exude a confidence in His Word that was supernatural.

From that time on, as we conducted each session, I knew that the members of our team were praying the entire time. Their eyes were open and they entered into the discussions, but they were still praying—especially for this woman. As the weeks progressed, the team noticed something happening. She was getting quieter and quieter, arguing less and less!

Faith in God's Word was just as important as prayer in this situation. Had we gotten defensive and argumentative, the whole group would have questioned our motives and our message, not just one argumentative person! However, confidence in God and truth allowed a calm, deliberate spirit to prevail in us. We were there to serve truth, not to argue about it. So that's what we did, all the time praying that God's Spirit would cut to the heart with His Sword.

For us, the turning point became evident one evening when this former antagonist calmly and quietly participated in the study. As it ended, she asked if we would recommend some good Biblically-based sources to study in preparation for the next session! God had worked mightily—in us and in her!

People with *shepherding* hearts and capabilities are also vital in this evangelistic ministry. Remember, our goal is not merely to evangelize, but to disciple (Matthew 28:18-20). Included on the ministry team should be those willing and able to go past the evangelism stage and take new believers through the other steps of discipleship.

How many believers should be on your ministry team? That depends in large part on the size of group with which you expect to work. In our experience, we have found the following ratios work well:

Number of Nonbelievers	Ministry Team Size
3-6	2
8-10	4
12-16	6
18-24	8

CHAPTER NINE

Prayerfully Planning

Once a ministry team has been formed, that team should meet regularly for three purposes. First, they should pray together. Second, they should review the principles and practices involved in evangelizing with a theocentric, chronological approach to the Scriptures. Third, the team needs to decide on some of the practical details connected with the study.

Some of these details are the location, starting date, time, schedule and agenda of the chronological Bible study. As far as location goes, we have found meeting in a home of one of the team members who lives in the neighborhood works well. This is especially true when the neighbors have been in the home often and are already comfortable in that setting. For sake of continuity and consistency, it is best to meet in the same home as much as possible.

Strive to meet weekly for the chronological study. This has been by far the best arrangement for us. However, we have had some groups whose schedules did not allow weekly meetings. For them, we found it possible to meet every other week without losing too much continuity in our discussions. Meeting any less frequently will make it very difficult for people to follow the flow of thought in the study.

One group I led tried meeting twice a month on the second and fourth Thursdays of the month. However, the people in the group asked to meet more frequently and adjusted their own schedules in order to do so. They recognized they were not benefiting as much as they wanted, especially when there were three weeks between sessions because of a five-Thursday month.

Here is a study session agenda that we have found works wonderfully for us in our evangelistic studies. Of course, the meeting times are sometimes different, but our schedule usually follows this pattern.

7:00 - 7:30 p.m.	*Social time* People coming in, standing around in the kitchen talking and eating munchies
7:30 - 8:30 p.m.	*Study and discussion time* (For some studies, this has been scheduled as a one and one-half hour block)
8:30 - 9:00 p.m. (or so!)	*Social time* People standing around in the kitchen talking and eating dessert

Holding to the agenda is necessary. You always want to end the study time on schedule, so the people attending feel they are able to depend on you. Those who have baby-sitters at home or who need to get something else done that evening like to know they can count on the announced agenda.

Do not overlook the importance of the social times sandwiching the study session. The pre-study social time allows people to become acquainted with one another, catch up on "the news" and be put at ease for the evening.

The time after the study is an important occasion for people to continue discussing the ideas that came up in the study, only in an even less formal setting. It is also an important ministry time, when people want to share one-on-one how something said during the study impacted them or ask questions about issues that may have been on their minds for many months, or even years.

CHAPTER TEN

Prayerfully Inviting

When the details and logistics of the study have been planned, everything is in order to start inviting your neighbors. Preferably, invitations will be extended about 4 to 6 weeks before the study is scheduled to begin. Not only does this help people fit the study into their busy schedules, but also it allows for followup and reminders of the invitation.

Personal conversations are the best method of initially inviting people to the chronological Bible study. Letting the subject come up in the middle of a "neighborly chat" keeps it on a personal, relational level. You may want to follow up with a postcard or a newsletter, but start out with the personal, face-to-face touch.

Some people will surprise you by asking if they can bring a friend, neighbor on the other side or relative along with them. Obviously, reaching out is what this is all about, so the answer will be "Yes!" in almost every circumstance.

As you invite these neighbors, there are some considerations to keep in mind. First, do not ask for an RSVP or any commitment from them. Keep all the pressure off them and put it all on the ministry team. Make sure the team makes all the commitments and has no expectations of the people who are invited. It doesn't make sense to ask for commitments from them when they do not yet know what it will be like!

Second, don't let rejections bother you. They will happen. For one reason or another, not everyone will be willing or able to come to the study. They may have major scheduling conflicts, or they may not be ready for this type of event—yet! That's fine. There are plenty of others in whom God has been working and who will be eager to come. Those who do come are those with whom God has given you the Bible study ministry at the moment.

Third, don't invite believers who are not on the ministry team. This is an evangelism outreach ministry, not a church meeting. Don't have believers taking up space where nonbelievers could be. It is tempting to do so, just to make sure the seats are filled. However, speaking from experience, you will probably regret yielding to that temptation. One situation you do not want to create is when the nonbelievers feel outnumbered and "ganged up on" by believers in the study. Avoid it at all cost.

The most frequent question I am asked in my seminars on conducting evangelistic chronological Bible studies is, ""How do you get all these people to come?" There are three primary reasons why people come to these studies in response to the invitations of ministry team members.

First and foremost, people come because of the *relationship* they have with the person who invited them. Very few will respond to the invitation of someone they don't know. That shouldn't surprise us. We operate in the same way. When was the last time you attended an event because a stranger asked you to come?

Second, people come because we tell them this is a study in which we will be *learning about who God is*. This touches a cord in many hearts. Many folks are aware of how ignorant they are about God. Like the Athenians, they have an altar in their hearts "To An Unknown God" (Acts 17:23). When they are given the opportunity to learn about Him, their curiosity is piqued and they respond positively.

Notice that this is one of the first commitments we make to neighbors, that we will be "discovering God." We are promising to be theocentric in our approach, and we better keep that promise.

Third, people come because we tell them we will be learning about God together *by studying the Bible chronologically*. Once again, this interests many who recognize their Biblical illiteracy.

We must remember that many of our neighbors have told us or others something like this: "The Bible? Sure I've read the Bible. It's so full of contradictions and fairy tales nobody would be a fool enough to believe it!" However, they know and we know they are lying. Usually they have never read the Bible. Often we find out they have never even owned one!

The same ones who make such brazen statements are those who come to *Discovering God* Bible studies. Why? Because it gives them an opportunity to find out what the Bible says without admitting they were lying. They may come with a gruff, defiant attitude on the outside, but the fact that they have come tells us there is an inquisitive mind and a crying heart on the inside. God is working in their lives, and He has seen fit to use us as His tools!

This, then, is a second commitment we make to those we invite. We promise them that we will look at the Bible in a chronological fashion to see how God has revealed Himself there. We must keep that commitment.

What causes people to keep coming after the first session or two? The same elements: relationships, focusing on God and looking at the Bible chronologically. Keeping our promises.

The relationships deepen when we start looking into the Word of God together and become fellow truth-seekers. There is something about joining hand-in-hand on a quest for God which forms bonds that become hard to break.

Many are eager to learn about God, in response to His drawing grace. However, they will depart quickly if we fail to keep our promise and start shifting our focus to anything other than God.

If our sessions become occasions for promoting a church or a preacher or a pet idea, the neighbors will scatter in the wind. That's not what brought them, and it won't keep them.

As we continue to look at the stories of the Bible chronologically, attendees get excited. Not only can they understand what the Bible is saying, but also it relates to modern, everyday life! God's Word actually deals with questions that have been on their minds most of their lives! How much better can it get?

CHAPTER ELEVEN

Prayerfully Conducting the Sessions

Have a Get-acquainted Session

Those who respond positively to your invitations may be willing to come to the Bible study, but that does not mean they have no doubts, hesitations or questions. In addition, not all your neighbors know each other, even though they may all know you.

For these reasons we have found it helpful to set a time when those planning to attend the study can get together, get acquainted with each other and find out in more detail what will be involved in the chronological Bible study. So we like to plan an ice-cream social, a picnic or some other special activity, just to get things started on the right foot with the whole group.

This get-acquainted time will be mostly informal, a social evening where people just talk with each other and become comfortable. However, at some point in the evening everyone gathers together and we accomplish three goals.

First, we describe for the group what the studies will be like. We reaffirm our commitment to learn together about God by looking at the Bible in chronological fashion, and we describe what that means.

Second, we go over the Introductory Matters material in the *Discovering God* study. This gives insight into the different perspectives we can have of the Bible and lays down the ground rules we will follow in the study.

This is a vitally important time. For example, the first guideline we establish is that we will study the Bible as being true. We point out that this does not mean those attending must accept the Bible as truth. It does mean that I, the leader, accept it as absolute truth. Also, it means that the group will assume the Bible is true for purposes of our study and discussion.

When we actually start studying the Bible, I have often had occasion to bring the group back to this and the other guidelines we established before the study began. When someone declares they don't believe what the Bible is saying at some point in the study, my response is simply, "That's fine. However, we established that we will study the Bible as true for purposes of our discussion, so that's what we will do."

Our job is not to convince them that the Bible is true. Our role is to present to them the truth of the Bible. Many times, the ones who start declaring openly and loudly that the Bible is false in the first sessions of the study end up talking about it as the truth near the end. This change occurs, not because we convinced them, but because God's Spirit persuades them of the truth of His Word as we open the Word with them.

Our third goal in the get-acquainted time is to give opportunity for the neighbors to ask their questions about what the study itself will really be like. They may wonder if they are allowed to bring a certain Bible version or worry because they don't have any Bible to bring. They may wonder if children can be present or if childcare will be provided. Any number of issues may be brought up. The more openly and confidently you handle them at this session, the more comfortable the people will be when the actual study begins.

Use Ice-breakers

Before each session actually started, one of our hosts impressed me with his ability to put the neighbors at ease with ice-breakers. During the pre-study social time, he had a whiteboard set up in the kitchen/dining area with a question or a fun assignment for everyone to fulfill. Just before the study began, this would become the basis for a group activity.

One evening the assignment was to think of three statements about ourselves, one of which was false. When the group sat down in the living room, each person related the three statements he or she had prepared. The group then tried to determine which statement was false. Not only was this a lot of fun, but also we learned a great deal about the people in our group that night! It was an invaluable time for our ministry team, enabling us to know better how to serve.

Have Guided Discussions

The surest way to drive everyone away from the studies is to turn them into lectures about God or the Bible. Not only will that approach make them feel like they are in school again, it will prevent the ministry team from learning all they can about those who are at the studies. It is in the questions and discussions that we find out where people are really at in their understanding and acceptance of Biblical truth about God.

So tell the people from the start that this will be an interactive time. Encourage them to ask questions and add ideas. When they do ask questions, be willing to admit that you don't know all the answers. If the question is worth pursuing, offer to investigate it with the questioner personally. What a great opportunity to deepen that relationship and model personal Bible study!

Don't feel the need to answer all the questions, even when

you know the Biblical answer! Let nonbelievers struggle and search. Give them the opportunity to find the answer for themselves. They may need some help and guidance, but let them be involved. That way the answer will be *their* answer, not yours!

I often put off questions for weeks, telling the questioners that we will be coming to the answer down the road. Of course, at those times I must make sure I deal with the question when the time is right.

One way in which we encourage group participation is by asking for volunteers to read the verses we are about to discuss. They like to do so. In fact, we often have several people start reading a verse at the same time. There is something about having them read verses that seems to make them more comfortable about asking questions and offering ideas.

One word of caution about this: never ask for any particular person by name to read a passage of Scripture. Some are deathly afraid of reading in public. In fact, some adults can't read at all. The last thing you want to do is drive them away because you have embarrassed them publicly. When leading a study, I always ask for volunteers in the same way, "Would someone please read Genesis 1:1?"

By the way, it is always good to have extra Bibles available for those who don't own one. Again, do everything you can to make them feel comfortable. They will be discomfited soon enough by what God reveals to them in His Word about their sin! Our desire is to make them comfortable in every other respect so they can focus on and be consumed by their spiritual discomfort—until they find the solution in God through Jesus Christ.

Avoid a "Church" Atmosphere

You may want to begin each study session with a brief prayer. This can have a powerful, positive impact on the nonbelievers present. Prayer thanking God for revealing Himself in His word helps to reinforce in their minds the purpose for which you have gathered and the grace God has shown to all by making Himself knowable. Prayer asking God to help everyone understand His word as it is read and discussed is an effective means of helping everyone realize that all are completely dependent on Him for the privilege of knowing Him.

We have also taken a few moments at the beginning of some sessions to pray for attendees with special needs of the moment. This may be someone who will be having surgery in a couple of days, or one whose relative just died. Such occasions can be highly effective in showing nonbelievers that we really care about them and their heartaches or joys. They also see readily the fact that the God we worship is highly personal, such that we can take our burdens, sorrows and happiness to Him. Once again, prayer on these occasions expresses our total dependence on the sovereign Lord.

However, a word of caution is in order at this point. Be careful to avoid creating or allowing a "church" atmosphere that will scare away many nonbelievers. This may be a Bible study, but it is for nonbelievers. Remember, they are at the study to learn about God, not to worship Him. If you stick to the stated purpose of the study, learning about God and getting to know Him, many of those attending will be worshiping Him soon enough.

The same principle applies to the use of music in connection with the study. At times we have played a song from a CD to open or close our study session, when it fit perfectly what we discussed and was understandable by everyone present. Hardly ever have we invited the group to sing Christian songs together, for the simple reason that the nonbelievers have never heard most of the songs before. The one exception may be if the group is meeting near Christmas and everyone knows some good Christmas carols.

They may enjoy singing a couple—especially if the lesson is about Christ's birth!

The idea is to be sensitive to your audience. Don't scare them off by opening every session with several Christian songs they have never heard before. Neither should you have a long prayer time that makes them uncomfortable and feeling like you have roped them into a church service that was not part of the bargain.

CHAPTER TWELVE

Prayerfully Concluding the Study

At the end of our *Discovering God* Bible study we have a summary of the entire study in 24 paragraphs, one for each session. After the study is completed, we meet one more time as a group for this wrap-up time. It is always one of the most special times we have.

Our custom is to sit around the living room and hand out the summary paragraphs on slips of paper to those in the room. Each person reads one paragraph in the order in which the lessons were covered. When a paragraph has been read summarizing that particular session, we stop and let the group remember and relate to each other what they especially remember from that lesson and how it impacted their thinking and their lives.

What a powerful time! Tears are often shed, laughs are always shared, and the impact of the entire study is multiplied.

However, this time is not just for looking back. The ministry team should have developed a course of action before this evening to continue ministering to the people who attended the study. It may include a followup study for those who trusted Christ during the chronological study. Whatever it involves, it should take into account where the people are at spiritually and what special relationships have developed during the study. Often, the people will almost demand that there be a continuation of ministry, especially if the relationships have deepened around the Word of God as they should.

One possibility for which the ministry team should be prepared is the neighbors' desire to have more evangelistic studies! We have had three men come up separately on the same night during the social time after a summary session and ask if it would be possible to repeat the study. Each of them said they had 20 to 30 friends they knew would come. That was somewhere between 60 and 90 people to whom we had the opportunity to reach out!

CHAPTER THIRTEEN

Prayerfully Following Up

Followup starts while the Bible study is in process. The ministry team should always be watching for the "natural" friendships that develop between the team members and the neighbors attending. These friendships should be pursued even outside the study sessions.

Be alert to the special interests of those who are attending the study. Find out their hobbies, special activities, the books they read, the sports they enjoy. Make arrangements to participate with them in some of their favorite activities, one-on-one or couple-with-couple. These times will become occasions of highly effective ministry, especially as the relationships grow deeper.

By the time the study is nearing an end, the team should have a fairly good idea of where people are at in their relationship (or lack of one) with God and who gets along well with whom. The "shepherds" on the ministry team may want to form small groups with the new believers, helping them along in the faith and incorporating them into the body life of the church. New believers may also be guided into a new believers' Bible study with others who have been reached through the church's outreach ministry.

Those who have not yet professed Christ but are still interested may be helped by setting aside several weeks to discuss their questions, doubts and hesitations. This may be done on a more personal level in their home, or perhaps in a smaller group than attended the chronological study.

The important point is, don't let these people fall through the cracks. Even the new believers who start attending church should be cared for on a more personal level. Just because they are attending church doesn't mean they are being shepherded as they ought. Remember, your privilege and responsibility is to make disciples, not to be satisfied with converts.

CONCLUSION

Oak Trees or Squash

Many decades ago, the president of Oberlin College was asked by a student at the school if it would be possible to take a shorter course than the regular schedule offered. His reply was, "Oh, yes! But then it depends on what you want to make of yourself. When God wants to make an oak, He takes a hundred years, but when He wants to make a squash, He takes six months."

You probably realized much earlier that the theocentric, chronological approach to evangelism is one that takes considerable time and effort. It does not strive to persuade people to trust Christ the first week of the study, or the second or third or fourth! It recognizes that they need a foundation of truth to be laid down for them first—truth about who God is and what He has done.

When that foundation has been laid and the background is grasped, those who trust Christ do so with much more understanding and much greater conviction concerning what they are doing. They are much less likely to be like the rocky soil in which the seed was sown, sprang up quickly and died just as rapidly because it had no root (Matthew 13:5-6, 20-21). They have had every opportunity to investigate, question and consider the truth presented in the chronological Bible study. The truth has had occasion to take root in their lives as the Holy Spirit wielded His sword in their hearts, session after session.

I say these things to leave you with some thoughts that I hope will encourage you. As you embark on the venture of helping people discover God through chronological Bible study, don't try to rush them into making decisions for which they are not yet ready. Don't take on the unnecessary and illegitimate burden of responsibility for how many people trust Christ or when they do so. Your role is to confront people with the truth. It is the work of the Holy Spirit to convince them of that truth and regenerate them. Let Him do His work in His time.

So be patient with the study, the ministry team and the non-believers who come. Be confident enough in our sovereign God, His word and the ministry of His Spirit to calmly and prayerfully serve up His truth to those involved in the study, week after week after week. You will see results. My prayer is that those results will be oak trees rather than squash, because of your willingness to be a patient, persistent vessel in the hands of our great God, making known His glories to a needy world.

Discovering God

Discovering God is the theocentric, chronological Bible study developed by James Odens, author of *Lighting the Way to God*, for use in evangelism. Materials available for *Discovering God* include the Leader's Guide, the Learner's Workbook, and color PowerPoint pictures or overhead transparencies.

For information on these materials and how you can order them, check out our web site at www.tcbs.org or contact us at:

TCBS Inc./PAGE Ministries
4233 Edgemont Street
Vadnais Heights, MN 55127-7946
(612) 414-7029
E-mail: PAGE@tcbs.org

Have a Conference on Evangelism in Your Church

James Odens, author of **Lighting the Way to God** and the **Discovering God** chronological Bible study, is available to conduct Conferences on Evangelism in churches serious about reaching this post-Christian generation with the gospel of God. For more information and to arrange for a conference in your church, go to our web site (www.tcbs.org) or contact:

TCBS Inc./PAGE Ministries
4233 Edgemont Street
Vadnais Heights, MN 55127-7946
(612) 414-7029
E-mail: PAGE@tcbs.org